PARAPROFESSIONAL COLORING BOOK

THIS BOOK BELONGS TO

_____

_____

Thank you for purchasing this coloring book.

Being a Paraprofessional can be stressful. Coloring as an activity has scientifically shown to promote mindfuless and reduce stress. So, enjoy mindfulness and relaxation with this brilliant anti-stress therapy.

Color Test Page

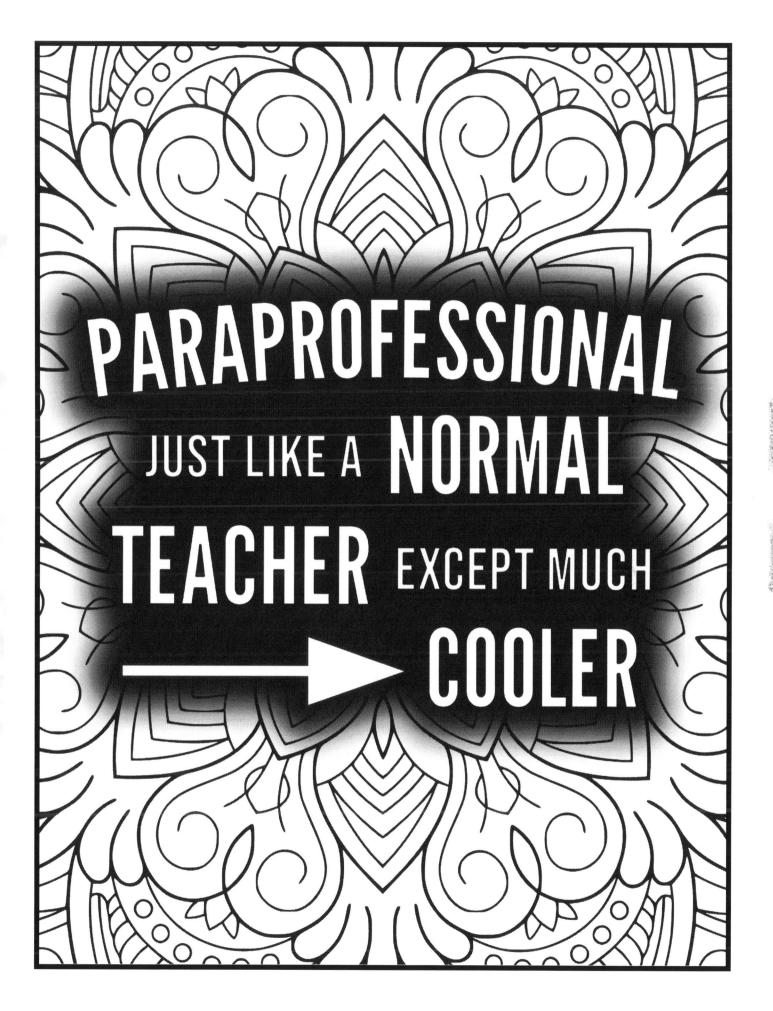

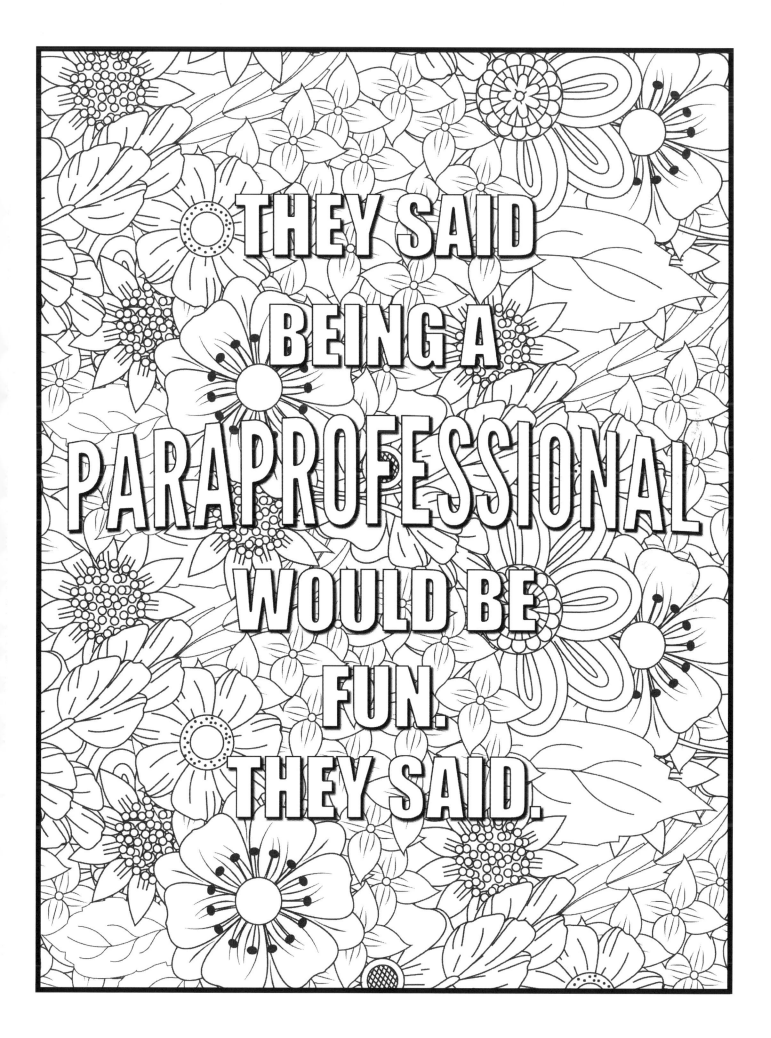

PARAPROFESSIONAL LIKE A SUPERHERO ONLY REAL

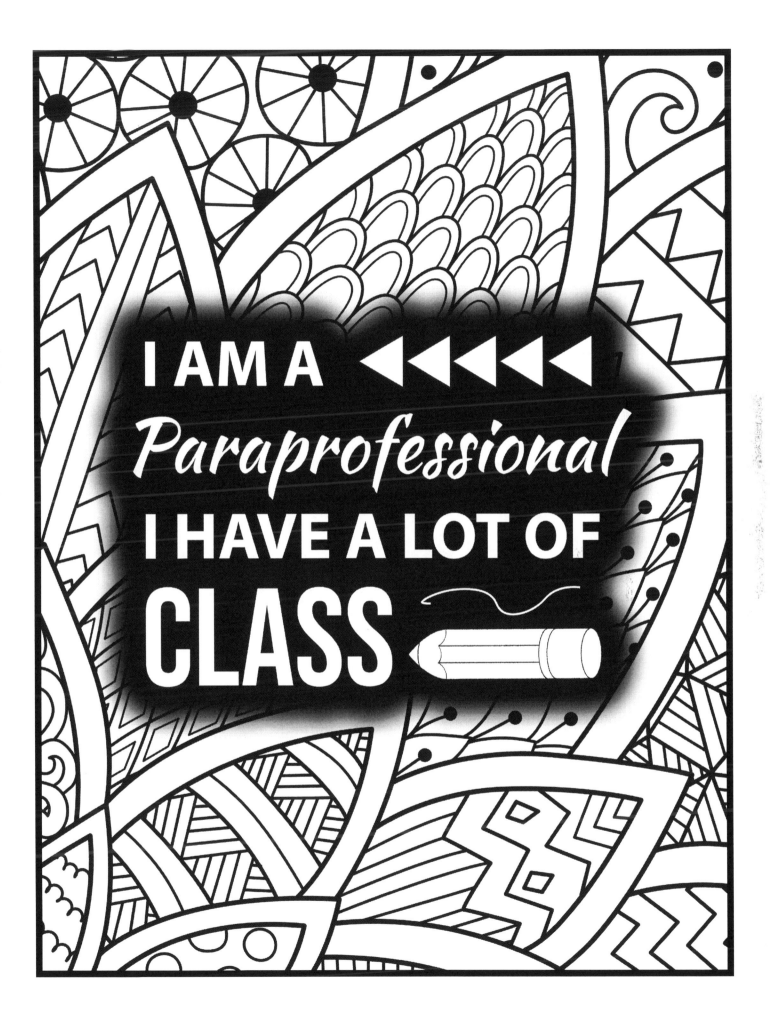

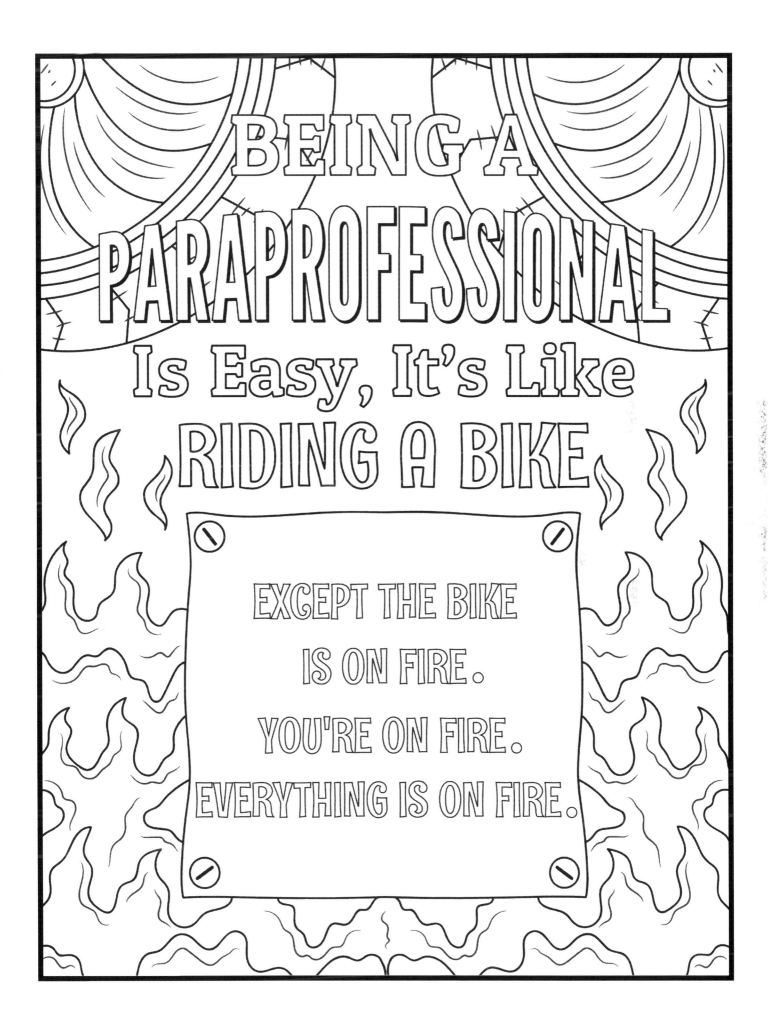

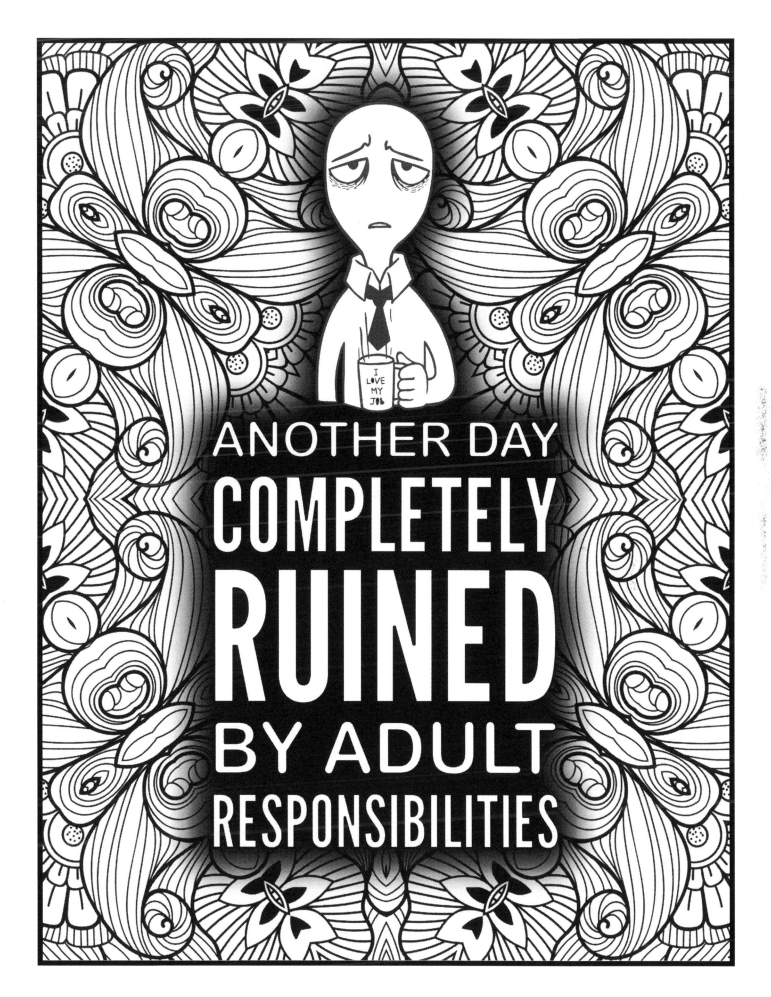

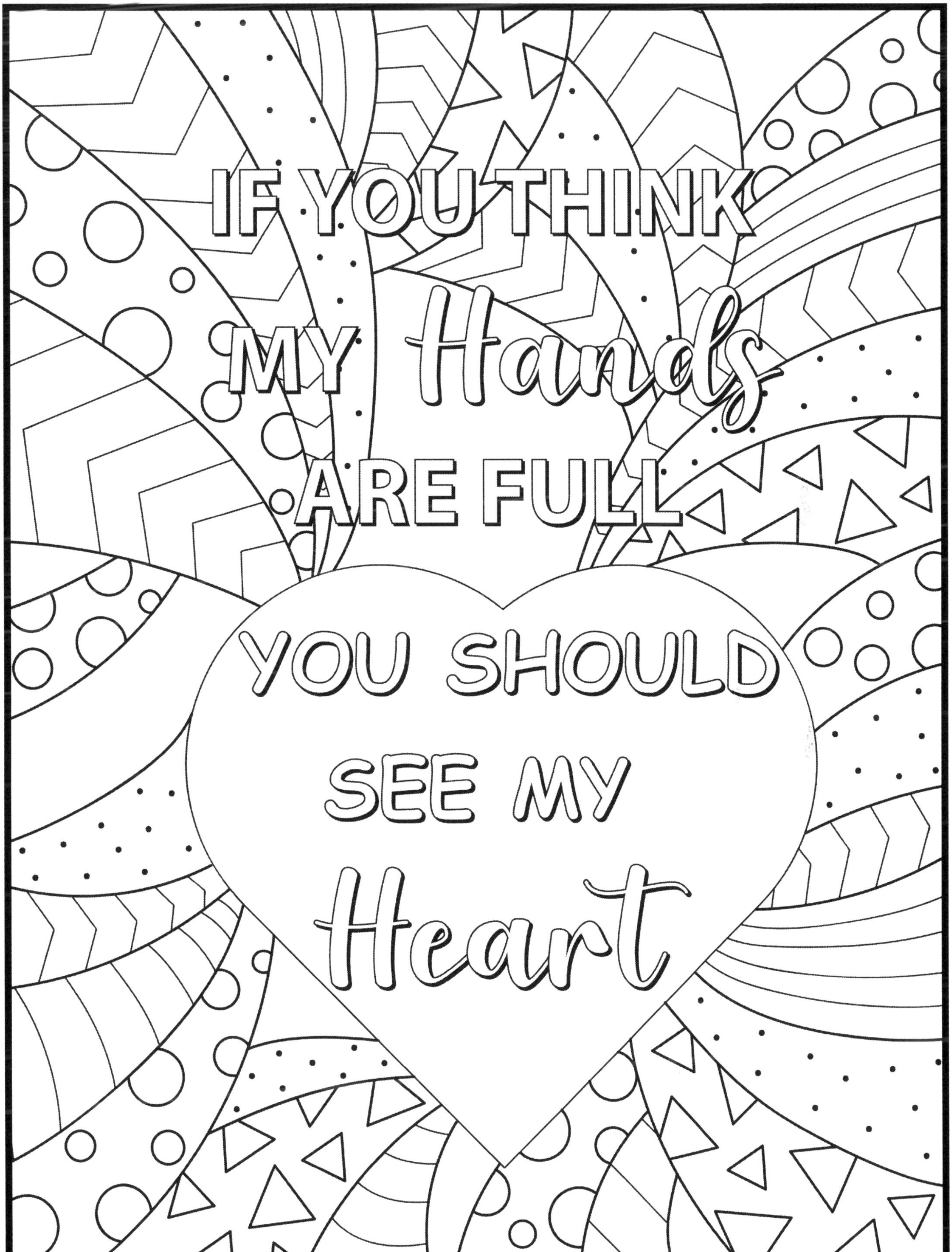
IF YOU THINK
MY Hands
ARE FULL
YOU SHOULD
SEE MY
Heart

I USED TO HAVE A

LIFE

BUT I DECIDED TO BE A

PARA

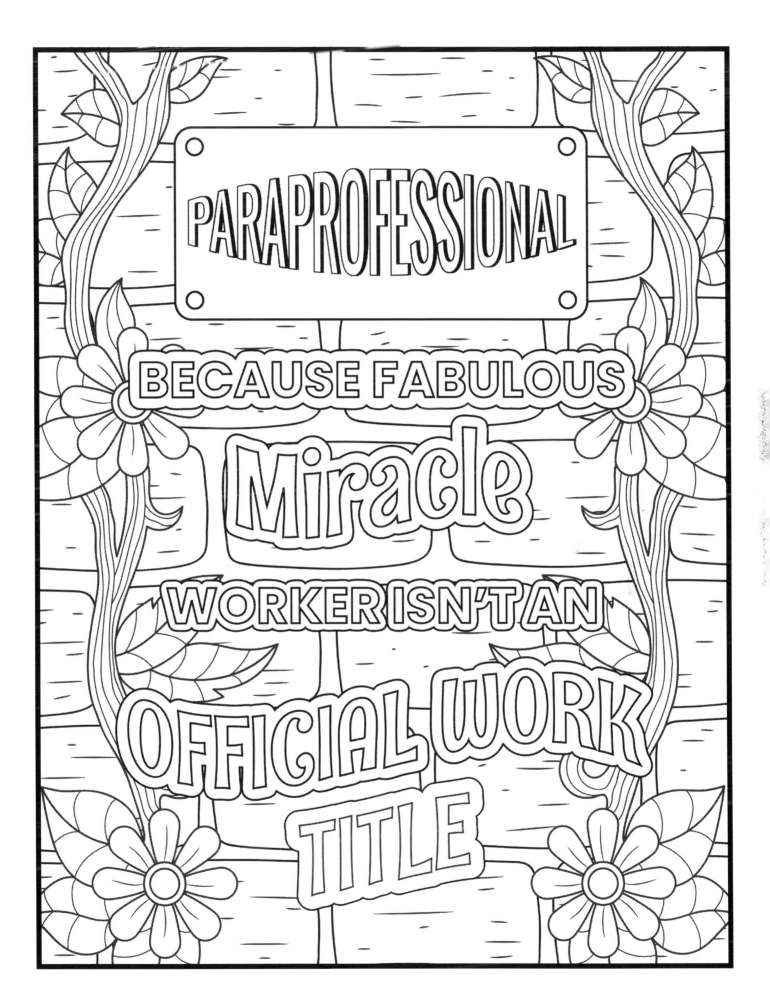

Hope you liked this coloring book.
If you did, check our
Paraprofessional Activity Book,.
By: Npvhtisa Publication

Made in United States
Orlando, FL
09 December 2024